Winner of the 2016 Cave Canem Poetry Prize

SELECTED BY KWAME DAWES

Inaugurated in 1999 with Natasha Trethewey's *Domestic Work*, selected by Rita Dove, the Cave Canem Poetry Prize is an annual first-book award dedicated to the discovery of exceptional manuscripts by African American poets.

Founded in 1996 by Toi Derricotte and Cornelius Eady, Cave Canem Foundation is a home for the many voices of African American poetry and is committed to cultivating the artistic and professional development of African American poets. The organization's community has grown from an initial gathering of twenty-seven poets to become an influential movement with a renowned faculty; a high-achieving fellowship of more than four hundred; and programs delivered in New York City, at the University of Pittsburgh (Pittsburgh and Greensburg), and nationally.

www.cavecanempoets.org

BEGIN WITH A FAILED BODY

BEGIN WITH A FAILED BODY

Poems by Natalie J. Graham

The University of Georgia Press | *Athens*

Dear Scott —
How lucky to have
met you and hear your
work. Thank you —
Natalie

Published by the University of Georgia Press
Athens, Georgia 30602
www.ugapress.org
© 2017 by Natalie J. Graham
All rights reserved
Designed by Erin Kirk New
Set in Garamond Premier Pro

Most University of Georgia Press titles are
available from popular e-book vendors.

Printed digitally

Library of Congress Cataloging-in-Publication Data

Names: Graham, Natalie J., author.
Title: Begin with a failed body : poems / by Natalie J. Graham.
Description: Athens : University of Georgia Press, [2017] |
    Series: Cave Canum Poetry Prize
Identifiers: LCCN 2017008992 | ISBN 9780820351209 (softcover :
    acid-free paper) | ISBN 9780820351193 (ebook)
Classification: LCC PS3607.R3465 A6 2017 | DDC 811/.6—dc23
    LC record available at https://lccn.loc.gov/2017008992

For Jo Ann Woods Graham

Contents

Foreword

Some of my worst wounds
have healed into poems.
A few well-placed
stabs in the back
have released a singing
trapped between my shoulders.
A carrydown
has lent leverage
to the tongue's rise
and betrayals sent words
hurrying home
to toe the line again.
—LORNA GOODISON

When the meaning of sweetness for a child who is poor, who wears worn-out shoes, and who repeats her Sunday clothes each Sunday is ambiguous and almost diabolical, we know we are entering a world of contradictions and haunting and memories that are never free of a certain trauma. From the first notes of her collection *Begin with a Failed Body*, Graham reminds us that memory is both disturbingly persistent in its accuracy and profoundly unreliable in its details.

I have of late been paying attention to how women of color are writing their bodies and about their bodies in poetry, and while this is not new—after all, it is what Maya Angelou, Gwendolyn Brooks, Lucille Clifton, Lorna Goodison, and Audre Lorde, to name a few, have been exercised by—what we see here are poets who have welcomed the gifts handed to them by their foremothers ("my wounds have healed into poems" [Goodison]) and have arrived at a poetics of defiance, authority, and sophistication that we will do well to note and celebrate.

For Graham the body that "fails" is her body, and in owning this body, beginning with it, she embarks on a journey that is about retrieval, reclaiming, and yes, healing of not just her body but of the bodies of those who have been wounded and broken:

Then, one day my dignified body
will tell nothing at all.
("The Palm Beach Story")

Graham, though, is not a blind optimist. Indeed, she is one who is willing to ask and leave unanswered the hard questions about the legacy of hurt in the bodies with which she peoples this collection. I am encouraged by the honesty in this uncertainty.

In the first of the two movements that make up the collection, Graham seeks her grounding and foundation in the wisdom that one can glean from the dignity and failings of family, and by family we do mean the parade of aunts, cousins, uncles, and parents (as well as the "fake" aunts and uncles) and the army of people who mark the community. She understands that the handling of the details of those she writes about with fascination and care is what turns an ordinary scene into something arresting. Whether it is the quick frown of an uncle in his alligator leather boots slick with rainwater when he hears Wilson Pickett sing of the "all night groover" or the wisdom of the dead Uncle Bubba whose words come to the speaker while he lies all dolled up in the coffin:

> You don't take care of shoes when they worn out.
> They'll throw good money in a dead hog's ass,
> then be too broke to feed what they got.
> ("Uncle Bubba's Funeral")

In poem after poem, the black body is an object of abuse and an object of strained beauty. At times it must be reckoned with as a mutating entity:

> The black body becomes
> the carcass of an insect,
> splinters of branches.
> ("To Hurt You (Reprise)")

In her best poems, it is hard to miss her deft skill in pulling the historical and social realities that preoccupy her into the present day-to-day outworking of her place in the world. In "Certain Immutable Laws," on a trip through the Florida landscape, the speaker and her companion have seen the relics and ruins of a slave past. As they negotiate the long journey through the night, the fatigue they express is not merely a fatigue from sleeplessness but a deep fatigue in the face of history's unsettling legacies:

> At the edge of dawn the interstate lightens before us.
> Ahead, heat and light break into pools of imaginary water.
>
> Farther off, grief finds us weathered.

The splendid possibilities in that adjective "weathered" are wonderfully evoked here—at once worn out, marked by damage and decay, but also seasoned, strengthened, and by extension, prepared for the hardships ahead. This same weathering is what marks those of her people who continue to feed her sense of self and value. In "Song, without a Musical Note for My Granddaddy," the grandfather, who cares for the speaker as his "cockatoo" in a wintery Florida, pays a price for this tenderness, but he marks his life, at least according to his wife, by looking forward:

> You begged no more from this meager life,
> than to lean forward, to earn, to eat, though it bled
> you dry. Ma said you never looked back, as if,
> at turning, you might vanish into shreds
>
> when you trudged headlong into both wars.

For her, history is a place from whence to consider the present moment. She makes reference to historical figures and moments—slave auction blocks, Africans who cut off their legs to avoid enslavement, slave castles, the legacy of Jim Crow, and so on—all with an attendant question: Will these things be repeated? The promise is that having experienced these things in our past, we will no longer have to experience them in the future. This is the hope of being a "weathered" people. Yet one can't help but sense a quiet uncertainty in these articulations.

The mouth is one of the most evocative images that runs through the collection. A sensitive and enterprising reader would find great reward in tracing the ways Graham employs the mouth as object, as a kind of living dangerous part of the body. In "To Hurt You (Reprise)" she turns the mouth into a receptacle for song and not a giver of sound: "sing bright song into my dark, wet mouth." And then we observe her fascination with the idea of the mouth as a wound, and as a stand-in for a wound that is at once deeply sensual and hauntingly grotesque:

> there is a wound
> flapped open like a trout's mouth.
>
> Its tenderness surprises me.
> ("Underneath There Is a Wound")

The wounded body resurfaces later in her poem "Something Sacred," one of the most resonant poems in the collection for its treatment of sickness (cancer, in fact), healing, anxiety about death, and the possibilities of faith or faithlessness. This time, it is the doctors who can "put their mouths" on what appears to be a moment of healing. The act of "putting mouth on" is an African act of cursing, causing bad fortune to come on something when it is named and spoken:

> Later, in the chapel,
> her wet hair hovering like a storm cloud,
>
> she will try to become something sacred,
> rechristen herself something
>
> the doctors won't put their mouths on.

She renames the tumor, visions it as a fruit, as a pear, and in so doing she engages a new spiritual act upon the body—a rechristening—that seeks to turn the tumor into "something sacred." The body, even as it betrays her, can be made to be a holy entity. This is sophisticated writing:

> We become terrain, first a body,
> then a shrine,
> then a road marker
> furnishing a crowded landscape.
> ("The Way of the Shrine")

Graham organizes the collection around a series of segues that are so carefully created that the whole thing feels like a seamless conversation across a range of sensations and meditations. From a journey through a familiar landscape, she is "triggered" into remembering a churchgoing childhood where her memory is at once reliable and fruitful and yet fittingly unclear. Then she shifts to the people of that time who become relevant again in the present moment, characters like a lover or the mother who then consumes the final sequence of the first section of the poem. There is a sense of movement, and yet the echo of images, such as the mouth or the body as an eel or insects, is a kind of thematic assonance that allows the collection to feel whole and contained, a part of a singular narrative of sensation.

The second movement engages themes of faith and its decidedly fleshy expressions. She rewrites biblical narratives such as those of Judas, Ruth and Naomi, and Peter by somehow testing the emotional and psychological implications of these myths. Peter, for instance, returns to the same beginning, but this time as one who has had a kind of surgery enacted on him—he remains the stone, the rock on which the church is built. But Graham knows that the theology of Peter as the first pope is one that has been the subject of great debate. So for her, Peter is the stone—both a hardened man, a weathered man, and at the same time a seed. With Ruth and Naomi, we at least have the questioning of the role of the "redeemer husband" Boaz, and though Ruth hungers for an answer from her mother-in-law, who essentially "pimps her out," the answer from her mouth is unsettlingly conservative—her body, once filled, will lead a dotted line to a rabbi. Her purpose, then, is to continue the lineage.

When Graham begins to invoke the novel *Beloved*, by Toni Morrison, as yet another scripture of meaning and belonging for the bodies that she has presented to us in the work, she arrives at a conclusion that follows elegantly on the idea of the body as a shrine, or as above, the body as its own source of healing:

> The body doesn't hold hurt
> like that. The body saves us,
> even as we are dying, from the last futile pain.
>
> Finally, wonder.
> Wonder remains.

In "Death Song for Zong," she does not leave the biblical allusions but complicates the story of the ark, a narrative she characteristically hints at in a few earlier poems, by turning it into the slave ship, the Zong, one of the great monuments of evidence that has been left for those that have come after of the horror of that moral travesty called the slave trade. Very quickly, the myth of Noah is overtaken by the historical fact of the killing of sick slaves by the captain of the ship for the insurance that is promised. The poet then offers a prophecy, a clear statement that her poems represent—that the murder of these black bodies by drowning, and the same drowning of the many others before and after the Zong, will not be forgotten:

Death will not forget these bodies,
these parts of bodies,
these scattered colored things;
will thrum a call on a three-note string;
will bring the lull that water brings.

The collection then returns to the lyric exploration of the singular body, a body that has found meaning in the classical art of Western culture, as in the ways she creates two ekphrastic poems drawn from the sixteenth-century French painter Georges de la Tour's "Magdalen with the Smoking Flame." She speaks in the voice of the subject, and as with so many subjects, she speaks back to the painter, casting herself as a dangerous part of the desire that he fears. It is a sexual desire that, through the inclusion of the skull in the composition, becomes a fear of death. Magdalen, though, recognizes that these preoccupations belong to the artist and not to the subject, and in so doing, she gains a certain agency, which strikes me as Graham's point:

The painter exhausted his brushes,
rendered my shoulders bare,
loosened my hair
into a black river.

I cradled a skull scoured smooth,
doted on a flame with a dreary eye.
The wound endured the waiting.

Graham does the same with the varied biblical narratives that she examines, sometimes fascinated by gender but most often fascinated by the meaning of deity and the position of the human body in the face of the idea of God. Her final subject, though, takes her to Shakespeare and to Ophelia, who, in Graham's hands, seems like a woman tempting suicide rather than a woman reflecting back after crossing the line into death. I suspect that I am left with this sense of a woman on the edge because Graham is drawn to the most lively accounting of the death of Ophelia in Shakespeare's play—an account that is as fascinated by the place where she drowns as it is by the fact of her drowning. It is Graham's almost clinical accounting that reveals this tension between the blunt language of the "muddy end" and the touching suggestion that Ophelia is somehow returned to her essential watery self. Here is Shakespeare's treatment of the moment:

> There is a willow grows aslant a brook,
> That shows his hoar leaves in the glassy stream;
> There with fantastic garlands did she come
> Of crow-flowers, nettles, daisies, and long purples
> That liberal shepherds give a grosser name,
> But our cold maids do dead men's fingers call them:
> There, on the pendent boughs her coronet weeds
> Clambering to hang, an envious sliver broke; . . .
> (Shakespeare, "Hamlet," Act 4, Scene 7)

In Graham's hands this account is captured and extended by daring to enter, albeit tentatively, into the mind of her Ophelia:

> Even with the buzz and prick of summer,
> what thumped in her brain
> was not the pulse of a dark thicket,
> the frenetic crescendo of cicadas,
> but snippets of verse that sounded sacred.
> She turned away from noise,
> cooling her hem in the current,
> washing a hand over her face.
>
> Lit from within,
> she was a candle to the cerulean shadows,
> perched on the edge
> of a black tangle of climbing vines.
> She waited, a doll half wooden and half glass.

The pond that she enters is fecund with life, with mutations, and with a quality of rebirth and regeneration born of the act of taking us to the pond after the drowning has taken place:

> Later, the sky would shiver under autumn's black hood,
> all pinpricked iridescent, cold air floating
> in ghostly currents.

And then in the second Ophelia poem, "An Element of Blank (Ophelia Reprise)," Graham denies darkness, the black hood of autumn, as the equation that guides Ophelia:

Though she waited for night to whisper something tragic,
she would not incline her head.

And this is how she ends her collection. There is something tidy about this return to the idea of traveling through the dark—traveling all night across the Florida landscape—that begins the collection. Through a series of moments of darkness, the poet continues, and yet she remains defiant in seeking out the dawn in each of those moments of shadow. There is something entrancing about the futility of the act, something that speaks to the hope and despair of poetry.

Graham's intellectual tentacles are long, and her imagination is generous. She is constantly searching for something to pull into the body, to feed the body. Her verse is terse, marked by technical compaction, and yet it is simultaneously grandly encompassing and voracious in its interests. In her we have a poet acutely sensitive to the ways of the body, its betrayals, its pleasures, and its unknowable selves. She is an exciting new voice, but this claim of "newness" seems almost trite, as there is nothing "new"—at least not in the sense we might apply it to a novice's work—about the authority, wisdom, and daring we find in these poems.

KWAME DAWES

I.

Junior Choir Recessional

This is where you wait among the filthy hills
of sinking graves and broken stones,
sweating in a crimson, polyester robe,
where you wait for water to make
you clean, wait for the hunger to come and pass.

You ashy underneath, socks don't match, are dirty.
Same every-Sunday-dress don't fit, hills of graves, rumpled earth.
Black as a buzzard, marchin in a half-heeled shoe, shoe bout broke.
This old, dirty, bout-broke shoe, and you marchin, steady marchin.

Sing now.
Bread of heaven, bread of heaven, feed me.
Soul singin, lined with sweat, nothing to do but sweat.
Wait. Soul singin, *Feed me heaven bread*

Lord, this soul gon clap.
This wing gon flap.
This broke, blackbird will

wait. You gon wait for him,
here, under the trees.
He'll put a piece of candy in you,
sweeten that mouth.

Look. Here's the church,
aint no steeple. This is how you wait,
baby bird, mouth cracked for a worm.

Bread of heaven, bread of heaven,
feed me til I want
no mo.

The Palm Beach Story

I make room for him
on our dilapidated chair.
The world outside shuts up.
A reticent sky is not angry,
but the glittering dark
withholds a story.

On a cracked laptop
a kindly Uncle outfitted for service
dodges monochrome bullets.
They ping but do no harm.
He, too, is harmless.
This demi-charactère is rustic,
pas seriuex, un divertissement
without the usual shucking and jiving.
He'll bow and yessir, hat in hand,
in a train's cage, in the line of careless gunfire,
all the way through Dixie.

We make a sweet home.
I fix my mouth
to explain
the difference between
Uncle and Coon,
Mammy and Pickaninny.

I've been told of charity—
not letting the right hand know of the other.
I can pour until the blessing comes.

Then, one day my dignified body
will tell nothing at all.

The Florida Motel

American girls are better than cream
spills from the greasy jukebox
as the line cook, scratching
his muttonchops

with the edge of an egged-up spatula,
points to the motel where a girl could stay
if she didn't mind a parking lot lit
with a couple of ghosts.

The Florida Motel is haunted
by a sexy adolescent in black spandex and yellow flip-flops.
You'll find her sitting, bored on a slice of grass
like a dropped coin purse.

The other stalks the half-empty pool,
digging into dark with a splintered cane,
in front of a Mercury Grand Marquis
with a chocolate bowling-ball paint job.

He delivers lukewarm pickup lines
to unseen loiterers, tipping his derby down,
Mama, you so hot, got me
bout burnt to ash.

Leaping Fire in Princeville Park

Quinisha skinned a black matchbox to spark
the boil for Cajun crabs.

Hammers waited to crack the smoking shells,
and picks glittered for the slippery meat.

Cee-Cee Plankfoot's South Carolina Shag
was a salty toe-drag. She slid to the beat.

With her polished face flashing in the fire
and shadows crawling through the cobwebs of fog,

these blues could be epic.
Call her, *Ma*. Let her sing,

No east, no west, no sleep, no rest,
just God in the sky and my soul in my chest.

Ghosts, looking like fireflies, flicked their
cigarette butts asking, *Why we here?*

Palatka, Florida

She patches wilted boxers,
disinfects a tattoo he can't reach.

No city will be built here,
zoning restrictions won't allow it,
and if they did, he'd hate to lose
a damn good bait-and-tackle
for some Yankee bullshit.

Mama told her not to have nothing,
don't have nobody's nothing
if you can't keep it fed
and rubbed down on a cold night.

The water's bad here, something like radioactive.
She can't sleep for thinking about the water.

The oscillating fan shakes its rickety head.
She smoothes the raised black mane of a tattooed lion
and burns like Moses's bush, fueled at four a.m.
by God-knows-what.

Holiday Spread

A key lime pie faced a glum pound cake.
The pineapple-upside-down Bundt with cherry eyes
ogled a turkey glistening with sweat.

Aunts Yvonne and Carmen paraded their best daughters
by the fuming food. One will be a dentist by May.
The other toed the ground, readjusted a snug Christmas-tree sweater,
and traced multiple X's over the grinning picture of a black Santa.

Uncle Freddy's black alligator-skin boots flashed with rain,
as he tapped his foot to Wilson Pickett.
His graying head, behind tinted shades, tilted against a wall.
He mouthed the words, *Midnight mover and an all-night groover.*
He frowned a bit and patted his thigh, *Got to be a real soul pleaser.*

Baby Boy, who everyone agreed had grown the most since November,
popped mini brownies, boasted of back-cracking
a Bobcat lineman and the freshman he might have given a concussion.
Beneath a peach collar, the tattoo on his neck ruffled its feathers.

As older cousins eyed envelopes of money
and wrestled for couch seats in front of the TV,
a tree slumped in the corner without lights.

Uncle Bubba's Funeral

Mourners spilled into the dusty road,
jawing snuff and cackling
at the high-toned, Holy Ghost fuss
being made over a Micanopy pig farmer.

Still sleeping, Bubba looked
mean as hot grits, ready as ever to cut
a decent Christian any way but loose
with his good eye.

He weathered his black bones,
plowing a share of earth he didn't own,
drank water-milk and ate molasses bread,
pacing his packed-dirt floor.

The spit-shined shoes and glinting silver coffin
don't fit. I knew what he'd have said
about spending money
to outfit the dead.

You don't take care of shoes when they worn out.
They'll throw good money in a dead hog's ass,
then be too broke to feed what they got.

Fairy Tale

While Audrey Hepburn brandishes a drooping
Technicolor bouquet of violets,
sagging petals sluiced with rain,
capes and coats dash around the cinematic storm
and dip quickly into carriages.

Outside, three men lie crumpled in a Datsun flatbed,
eyes slits, bodies wedged between hot melons.
A woman stoops, pulling her bandana, a Haitian flag,
from her head. Her shadow, an uneven bruise
in the sand, is pierced with stakes of light.

Others pick tomatoes,
lob the orangey bulbous hearts
into half-cracked barrels bristling with splinters.
There is talk of work farther north.

On the abandoned set,
Hepburn pretends to be
a squashed cabbage leaf
writing the American epic.

Certain Immutable Laws

for David

I. There is no break in nature.

A coil of root lies at our feet,
listening like an upturned ear.
A young boy traces a stubby finger
along the Old Slave Market's wall
of broken shells and trumpet vines.
Castillo de San Marcos extends
its shadow into the water.

We quicken—having spent too much time already,
having meant only to stop for lunch—
up San Marco Avenue, past the Huguenot Cemetery.

II. Nothing passes from one state to another . . .

Later, the first spectacular dollops of summer
erupt on the ashy windshield,
and we listen to the rhythms of the cracked pavement.
We hammer home, the '47 Fleetwood an ark
for just us two. You say, *Woman, I'm tired.*

. . . without passing through all intermediate states.

At the edge of dawn the interstate lightens before us.
Ahead, heat and light break into pools of imaginary water.

Farther off, grief finds us weathered.

The months are long in this flat, hot state,
but they pass.

Raised for Testing

Gray dirt snaked under a covering of trees.
The descent felt steeper, turning off the last highway in town,
how the path to the old house sunk down,
and dirt rose, on both sides, cut with black roots.

Every summer our tan jeep, down on a dirt snake,
wound its way toward the old farmer,
the ice box, the washboard, the outhouse,
the tin tub, and the rabbits.

Past the sagging house, through the gate,
the yard opens to what should be wilderness
but is just more sky and the long rabbit house.

The old farmer talks about cotton money, coal money, railroad money,
and rabbit money.

You only enjoy the dollar you spend,
and the best dollars rabbit dollars.

The feedbag drags another snake behind us.

In the rows of steel cages hundreds of rabbits
thump soundlessly, soundless except for the thumping,
the rattling cages, the scratching, the cages not quite rattling but quivering.

If they hissed or squealed, I don't remember their rabbit noises,
just their mouths quivering, and their cages almost rattling,
and them thumping their jumpless limbs,
and the machine of cages quivering and scraping together.

Song, without a Musical Note for My Granddaddy

Knee-deep in heaped okra, who needed English?
The goitrous squashes sat by a rusted hoe.
You watched a doe-eyed Jesus with a servile hush,
then rapped the ground with your emphatic *Oh,*

well, Sir Lord, Amen! Squatting over russet
earth, you hoisted feed and reaped greens all week,
voice bamming the yard before you'd cross it,
singing about that lucky ol' sun rolling up the blue and back.

You begged no more from this meager life
than to lean forward, to earn, to eat, though it bled
you dry. Ma said you never looked back, as if,
at turning, you might wither into shreds

when you trudged headlong into both wars.
In a lockbox, under yellowed conscription tickets,
memories sat like a tangle of barbed wire,
dark as cropped thickets.

One torpid winter, 1982,
the windows were iced with Florida's first frost.
I was your baby bird, your cockatoo,
not knowing what would be the cost.

Vacation Bible School

A clapboard belfry and a bell with no rope to ring it
hung above the foyer in Fort Clarke Missionary Baptist Church.

In this house of vernacular architecture,
the amen corner did penitent sinners double duty
with a mourners' bench and a baptistery fed by an anointed garden hose.

In an alcove by the pulpit, a mother's felt hat
swayed precariously to the hum
of four robed deacons.

Outside, there was no verdant expanse
where manna might fall if money was tight,
just a dusty dirt-patch lined with card tables,

where the hospitality committee
sweated over miniature sweet potato pies
and pressed a hundred hot dogs into white bread.

The committee swatted flies and chatted vigorously
about the time Deacon McCloud brought his shotgun
and promised to send Elder Flemming right back where the devil brought him from.

What did I know then? I was still shouting *The Cosby Show*,
playing TV freeze-tag, tripping over an unstitched hem,
and ripping sashes off handmade dresses.

The Idea of Order

When I read "The Idea
of Order at Key West,"
I thought first
of the man
who hacked off
his own leg to keep
from being sold there.

In a certain backyard
his body still hangs
suspended by its canvas thumbs,
chin cut off,
ears missing,
Raggedy-Ann-red yarn
dragged out the cut throat,
fingers, shredded strips
of a burgundy cable knit.

Consider how much killing
and what kinds of dying it will take.
How must this potato sack of a man
be beaten, and with what,
before it is burned?

We call this pyre a blessing.
We say that we are safe.

Now the twigs will not snap beneath us.
Now our burlap scrap bodies, sewn together with mud, will not betray us.
Now we bathe in the swampy light at dawn.

We say the spirit will never dream its way back,
will never catch us
asleep.

But, Mama

In the vague slip of aging—
brown head slick as a baby animal,
nodding, swaddled—
lips blur, petals on the slack mouth,
teeth dim in the dark pitch.

Your hands fumbled, heavy and mottled,
dirty with work. Water spilled from cups
and change from a torn purse.

A storm's been gathering for months now.
The days stink with rain.

What did you say that meant? *God bless the rain;*
trouble find a way when there aint no storm.

The work? Picking okra, fingers wrapped in rags.
You were buying chocolate chip cookies.
Two wet dimes on the counter, a nickel on the floor.

Your body, a greedy temple,
creaked with uneasy worship.
What invisible part of it throbs,
cold beneath my tongue like a straight razor?

Already it fails, withering, delicate wafer.

To Hurt You (Reprise)

"The woman with the microphone sings to hurt you."
—from "Track 1: Lush Life"
by Jericho Brown

If I unravel this body
into a pool of black shimmering,

of ribbons, coils of dance, of flitting—

If I pull at this sturdy plank,
tear flesh to tatter, become flutter.

If I say, *Open your hand*—
If I say, *Here. Here*—

Your strong name
is in my mouth, *Daniel.*

Your body is a jumble, a swarm held together with light. I want
a tangle of glossy leaves scattering light. I want,

perhaps, to hurt your buoyant body as it rises, to make
you feel. I can't heal myself without cutting down branches.

Your hard body is a fountain
of metal arches, a stream of bright notes.

Open tender body, open hand, supple fleshy palm, bony wrist,
sing bright song into my dark, wet mouth.

The sturdy body cannot become ribbons,
this tender box must hold itself,
must quiet the water that is always opening into streams.

These wooden branches, rigid, scraping,
fearing shatter, brittle with rot, cannot unfurl.

The black body becomes
the carcass of an insect,
splinters of branches.

What Might Not Break Through

The night I left you, when the neighbors woke me
with an indecipherable shout and door slam,
we lay tangled on a sagging air-mattress.
Your computer's red light winked.
The heating unit shuddered as cold eased
under the duct-taped window.
Things seemed willing to settle
into the midnight hush.

I found myself standing,
facing a young girl cross-legged on embroidered sheets.
Her brown hands, cut with pale scars, fumbled
over pages in a large blank book, tearing each out,
the pages fluttering to a cracked wooden floor.
Her face lifted, as if I'd called out to her.
Her eyes were opalescent, like marble,
and her black cave-mouth gaped open.
As quickly she came, she vanished;

and I was back watching you sleep.
Cold shivered up from my feet on the blue tile,
and only then did I remember the uneven floorboards
of the room where I spent a summer as a child.
I listened to my cousin's story of how everyone is buried alive,
how it takes the body a full year to die
in the coffin, aware and unable to move.
Past the blindness of that rural night, the warm flicker
of his flashlight sifted through the dark,
and the momentary image of him flashed (was it imagined?)
as he leaned into me, lying propped up on one elbow,
a warm hand, foreign, sliding up my thigh.

Underneath There Is a Wound

There is a man who writes poems about letters
or poems that are letters from soldiers,

or who writes letters to the soldiers
who die with blank faces.

There is always another
blank-faced boy to forget.

Underneath this poem,
and listening to the man read his poem,
and forgetting,

there is a wound
flapped open like a trout's mouth.

Its tenderness surprises me.

My boy is tender for dead things,
whines for the gone life, lays a leaf over a cricket's carcass,
talks breath back into things that never were.

Seeing the socket where a fish's eye had been
at the dinner table,
the hole behind the eye,

I forget the soldier
who was not
a metaphor for loss,

the life behind the poem,
the wound and blank,
all of it—

I fail to remember.
I refuse to touch

another   mother's   flickering   body

even to warm mine.

Another blank-faced boy
dying, mouth open, still moving
his wasted body, shuddering
like a huddle of velvet ducklings.

The Way of the Shrine

after Juan Delgado

The imprint of his mother's body
on the hospital bed is a doorway.

So vivid, then gone, he says of her memory,
of her forgetting, first being a teacher,

then being, *then gone, an imprint.*
He sees them everywhere:

Two tomato slices on the almost empty plate,
wobbly highlighting in a book of Psalms,
the places her hands might have been.

He never said her body was a doorway.
He said that shadow is an imprint of the body.

I don't remember my mother
polishing her nails,
though I was old enough
to make memories.

Before the wake, my aunt says,
Make sure her lipstick is red.

I think she liked pink. I recall
the smell of her face powder. I think
I saw one of her fake eyelashes on the dresser,
the dresser with one door broken off. And wasn't the other door
half-hinged and one of the drawers inside also broken
and the brown curtains never quite shut
and the light coming through them slanting through dust
and the walls stained—

We become terrain. First a body,
then a shrine,
then a road marker
furnishing a crowded landscape.

Partial Afterword, Waffle House Hours

after Isabel Nathaniel

The Beholder: A Tale.
You promised partialness, quoted James,
The whole of anything is never told.

You wrote of domestic holdings:
a steady house bathed in temperate light,
a husband and wife's gentle breakfasting,
an interminable hush.

In the intensity of my three a.m. study,
the surroundings unfasten.

Sixteen Candles floats from hidden speakers.
Dingy magnolias swirl mercilessly.
Concentric shining sings
from the bottom of a coffee cup.
A white halter top burns behind glass.
Sounds vanish into a rusted drain.

My dark eel body
cannot find a moment of rest
in this deep sea.

Intersection

In the front yard, red,
limp azaleas,
in silent litany,
cluster for water.

Magnolia blossoms
shrivel, yellow.
Shrieking crickets scuttle
behind a battered mailbox.

As summer persists,
everything exaggerates.

Light splits darkened corners,
lines the wooden floor.
Selfish and unashamed,
I am jealous of your better daughter.

Even in August,
when I'd expect winter to hide
beneath the ground,
you look cold,

trembling and glittering
like some weak thing of God.

I spoon you diminished bites.
Smaller, you say.

Your stiff fingers, like matchsticks,
scatter across the sheet.

Though your body is a battleship
upon which night advances,
could you pity me, Mother,
cornered and nicked as a doorstop?

Revolving Door

Who'd ever thought this would be a tragedy?

Oh, honey,
            tragedy is inevitable.

And the mother was off and talking
about the Thanksgiving she sliced her finger
to the bone
            and bled through five ivory napkins.

You were happy enough to dive at him
like a hummingbird.

The daughter dissected artichokes.
Italy spilled across the kitchen table.
A two-bit album made a mess of empires,
glossy and flinging light like a revolving door.

What domesticity they feigned that summer.
Rain drilled the soil.
She sang, *Love is a constant sun,*
            and drank eaux-de-vie from a thermos.
Her heart glowed like an electric eel.

Then—
            Who knows, baby doll?
            These things happen when you shack up.

Mother did not think it could have been a natural ebb;
she had evidence, warned of doing the right thing the wrong way,
wagged a carrot pitifully.

Exposing wrinkled shoulders,
a bare turkey swam
the darkening sink water.

Domestic Figure

In the refrigerator,
near wrinkled artichoke hearts,
an eggplant flaunts
the grotesque anatomy of spoilage.

Outside, my father is on all fours,
rooting around in limey soil.
This is Florida, you said.
We must till. Expect fruit!

How industrious he is.
Soon there may be nothing
left of our yard
but black earth picked clean.

I imagine you nearer.
Our cupped hands suspend a secret
of useless passion.

Our poisoned enterprise floods with harsh light.
I suppose, in order to transcend, everything real
must be made of marble
and added to the list of statues.

In front of a fireplace,
your plate, untouched,
cools by degrees.

The First Hike

I carry the water
up the slanted, cracked path.

A surprise of milky quartz,
dandelions, and a hill of white clovers
collapse together in memory.

I consider my breath in the mountain air.
She calls me *romantic,*
in a bad way.

Water from the ephemeral lake
may hide under the rocked soil.

She clamps a husk of bark around my wrist.
Her boots chomp the black oak leaves
flooding the trail. *Last fall's fallen leaves*

is redundant. She gives every scatter of rumpled things a name.

Gentle Jeffrey—
she points at a pinecone
I'd stamped flat—*only becomes dominant in the worsening climate.*
You know naturalists call bad soil, stressful?

A tornado of flies.
An empty fire pit.

I sit on a slab of twinkling rock,
clack broken quartz in my hand like dice,
huff the thin air.

Judas Kiss

Judas was a skeptic.
Blood. Bread. Wine.
Everything tasted heavy.

The Sanhedrin scanned the feathered scriptures.

Jealousy fell on Judas like sawdust,
burned his eyes, lined his tongue
with wood.

Don't take yourself so seriously, the Sanhedrin said.

Poverty lit on Judas's shoulder,
its talons grazing the crease of his armpit.
It licked the crest of his ear,
singing songs to him that hadn't been written yet:
        One glad mornin when this life is over, I'll fly away . . .

The Sanhedrin fingered its tassels.

There was no escaping hunger.
Judas swallowed hard.
The moon touched him with light.
Night poured from his mouth.

Last Lament for Judas

Where you are going,
there is no light,
or the light will be so dim
that shadows will float above the ground
transparent as feathers,
bleeding, forever dark into dark.

Periodic shimmers
will give no warmth,
and though each slice of spilled light
will seem to be a cracked doorway,
it will fade as you approach.

Will you leave me though I give to you?

Love, you will fumble about
in that perpetual grayness,
not knowing whether the wilted leaf,
the shivering hand,
you hold is mine or another's.

Here is my hand beating limply.
Here is my hand that falls to earth,
pulled down by plain gravity.

Gallery Songs

for Cynthia

I. If you want to buy my wares . . .

In the gallery, *Desperation* and *Need* are not for sale,
neither is *Night's Mist,*

but you can buy *What Makes Love
Fade.*
            Come, see:

the crescent of her body in the clutch of need,

the drenched mop of her body
cutting the red flame with its shadows,

these small photos you can buy.

II. What Makes Love Fade?

Money or Lack, Noise or Silence,
I answer expertly.

I am a scientist, dissecting
this heart like a greasy frog,
handling its limp tubes
with my metal fingers.

III. Estas son las mañanitas . . .

You said my heart hopped
like a *rana* and sang me a frog song,
rubbing your fingers on me,
fingers that you think are crooked.

Sana, sana, heal, heal,
you sang, if not today, mañana,
rubbing your hands on me,
hands too small to hide a strawberry.

Despierta, mi bien, despierta,
I want to touch you
while you are wide awake
with my dirty mouth.

Jesus and the Prairie

She says, *You don't want to keep your body well.*

We are here together in the waiting.
When will we get there, Jesus?
She is not ironic.
We are waiting for an answer.
Where did you come from?
How did you get here?

This moldy room could be a gymnasium
or an abandoned museum.
I empty her plate of fish into the garbage.

I know my body. You have to know your body.
You should keep the body well, she says.
Do you want to get well?
None of this dying has beauty in it.

I say, *Remember the shivering crane on the prairie?*
Its terrible red eye, bloody patch of forehead, us thinking it must be a devil?
Her body tenses and quakes. Pain travels through.

Just don't seem right to be a lone bird. Birds flock, she says.

The pulse races before it slows, slows.

Any day now we'll split this ocean in half,
lunge beyond the caution ropes into a furious landscape
of dense whipping weeds,
shivering, racing into the cold, windless prairie.

Something Sacred

She wakes at the first slant of day,
dawn warming across the sky.

She'd dreamt of pools of black water,
greasing the edge of the world.

The sheet is bloody
with ink; the pen threatens,

like an uncapped syringe, to prick her.
She might have slept another fifty years

if this were a fairy tale.

A mango, a veiny plexus in her uterus,
the tumor is shaped like birth.

Hospital curtains blow up
like a skirt. Light opens and unfolds—

a lily fluttering on white linoleum.
She imagines escape by window.

Later, in the chapel,
her wet hair hovering like a storm cloud,

she will try to become something sacred,
rechristen herself something

the doctors won't put their mouths on.

Magdalen with the Smoking Flame

after Georges de la Tour, 1593–1652

I was a sparrow beating
feeble wings into the sun.
My blank sparrow eyes
knew nothing of waiting.
I was perfectly dead.

You weren't you, were gone,
had never been.
Your body was just another shadow
moving against me
in the darkening.

The painter exhausted his brushes,
rendered my shoulders bare,
loosened my hair
into a black river.

I cradled a skull scoured smooth,
doted on a flame with a dreary eye.
The wound endured the waiting.

Then, a moment of blasphemy—
how could I control the dreaming?
I was you, Dear.

Weak angels lurked,
hesitant to heal.
Gaggling sinners crushed
and shuddered forward.

One stretched long in my direction,

Master, my demons are gone.
Lover, is there blood in you? Touch me.

Is she the worst that has ever been?
What sudden trouble
could one woman make?

Magdalen with the Smoking Flame (Chiaroscuro Reprise)

after Georges de la Tour, 1593–1652

Flat feet and round face,
pinky nearly slipping

into the skull's socket
on the red lap.

Whole life spent for a fuel
that burns clean in the shrinking light.

These shadowy folds and drape of skirt.
That warm custard shoulder.
The fussing over another candlelit Mary.
The violence of private doubt.

We lose so much to shadow.
The eye strives to make it out.

Where does the light point?
Where is she leaning?

The Lord is near,
yet what feels nearer?

The image and the fact of the image and you, Georges,

the baker's son,

furious with desire,

tracing a rope,

trailing it into the shadows.

Cinderella Sends Her Godmother Away

I will never leave this house.

How I hated the company of women
and called my sisters wicked
when they tied down
my restless hands with work,
when they licked me
with their curses.

But, Keeper, all names are curses.

You know how my body
arches for the faithful,
brutal touch of almost family,
how the skin hollers to be rubbed
quiet with hurting.

Don't send your chariot.

Let me slip back into muddy dark.
Let midnight expose a dirt-born,
squared-toed monster
from which all pure hands shrink back.

The Temptation of Saint Anthony

Restorer of Lost Things, you resisted drowning,
turned from your reflection in Lisbon's rivers,
looked west, past the castle of St. George
waiting like a pup on the doorstep
                                    of God
for the sun to set the sky on fire.

In and out of love with everything, you held
yourself tight from the appearance of spoilage.
Seventeen, impervious and water-ready,
you sailed for Coimbra.

The streets of Alfama fell away, a dropped net.
You skimmed cold avenues and leaned
into holes in the ground, yearning to be burned
at the stake or pierced by lions.

You were an ark and the world was bankrupt.

How we imagine you were tempted—
an elephant trampling in tempera by the sea,
a fish, gondola, or cloven hoof in gold leaf
near a castle's ruins, a bare breast hanging
like an open eye in the dark.

I wonder, Fernando, surrounded by so much silence,
might the mind whorl itself into oblivion?

Might you have failed, lover of the cross,
dragging yourself above the flat horizon
like a dingy gull, needed forgiveness, sinking,
then rising toward heaven?

The Threshing Floor of the Redeemer

Each day begins with a single pull, then another sharper pull.

Ruth dislodges herself from the mirror of a dead soldier's armor.
She turns toward the room. Her new mother
pulls a ragged tool through graying hair.

> *Bitter woman, do you still crave your God?*

Ruth lifts a limp wing to see if it might still keep wind.
The mother bats at the wing, fiercely, then playfully.

> *You're foreign, but a pretty pearl. Even in famine*
> *the king survives. I'll explain God when your belly is full.*
> *Maybe, my God waits for you*
> *to suck chaff off the spilt barley until it opens to sweet.*

> *New mother, tell me what is this word, Ga'al.*

> *Where is your perfume?*
> *Catch your kinsman's bleary old eye,*
> *shining and full of drink under the tunnel of night.*
> *Soften the prickly bed he's made from piles of wheat.*

The bitter new mother turns the ragged tool on Ruth, like a scythe.

> *Daughter, your name means friend.*
> *Will you test me in this? This man will make*
> *you bear a lion. The lion will turn lust*
> *into blood and blood into praise.*

The mother taps Ruth's elbow, breast, thigh,
wondering if parts might be hollow enough to float away.

Mother, you are mine. If I do what you say,
will you tell me why your God made me
scour the land for the leavings?

The mother's mouth turns into something of a smile.
She sucks her teeth, shakes her head.

Daughter, there's always something left.
My God will make a rabbi from your dotted line.

Peter Prays after the Crucifixion

> But he replied, "Lord, I am ready to go with you to prison and to death."
> Jesus answered, "I tell you, Peter, before the rooster crows today,
> you will deny three times that you know me"
> —Luke 22:33–34

What a broken miracle I've become.
Rabbi, I squandered glory.

My velvet body, a spoiled peach,
gives way to sticky ruin in layers.

My spongy pith, withering rot,
calls to be fixed to a cross.

No carpenter.
My hands failed against planks in shame.

Rabbi, you cut me open, rooted out my wormy pit.

Ask me now. I answer well.
I rage and quiver for your refuge.

I will glut on ash, scrape myself on rocks.
Burn, glut, and scrape.

Look on this flesh, this hand, this broken bone.
Make stone. Make stone. Make stone.

Black Willow

How the body swells
with injury. Floods cankers
with clots and fever.
Gives over its weakest parts.
Licks its wounds with fire.

Its limbs are not arms.
The willow's buds cluster,
turn for sun. It weeps pitch.
Its sick black willow body
shudders in the prairie wind.

Cracked grey-black bark splits
from quick growth. This black willow
lets down leaves too soon.
Brittle limbs snap and scatter
without ever splintering.

The red-winged blackbird
builds nests in willow branches.
Abandons, rebuilds,
abandons. Rebuilds to keep
young from nursing flies with blood.

Naked, in a Stormy Passage

after "The Middle Passage" by Malcom Cowley and Daniel P. Mannix

The skin over their elbows
might be worn
away.

Sleep. Sleep without covering.

In a space
between,
the women wander,
right wrist to left wrist,
ankle to ankle.

Sleep. Forced to sleep almost
anywhere. The skin might be worn
as a covering.

The bare bones
allowed to wander
almost anywhere.

Two by two,
between decks, the women,
skin worn,
regarded as fair, sleep.

Sleep sailors.

Then, another, two by two—
then, another—
then,
in the space between
night and day,
sleep.

Soon all the slaves sleep.

To the bare bones, sleep.

Sleep, stormy passage.

Sailors, naked women, day,

sleep, sleep, sleep.

Death Song for Zong

I.
The death bleat throbs
in a blackened thumb.

With light reflecting off the fog,
there is no way to tell

that this is the last petal of night to fall.

Pain sucks the lights

down its smutty throat

with sharp breaths.

The raven has not returned.
The memory of its body beats
a greasy mirage of feathers in his hands
like a black heart.

II.
If only the covering of dark
could hide us below.

Too many black bodies
drinking down the water.

When the captain starts his killing,
it doesn't matter how much
water is left. Sick niggers die,
and they all sick

Death will not forget these bodies,
these parts of bodies,
these scattered colored things;
will thrum a call on a three-note string;
will bring the lull that water brings.

Announcement

One day the world stopped smiling for the boy,
hands refused to blink open and shut their hellos.
His grimy body stuck to their eyes, an overexposed photo
blacked by too much light.

> *Godawful thing to be no good at the life you got.*
> *Godawful thing to be forgettable and full of vinegar.*

That September an ashy tree lashed his back with shadows.
Two black pistols in hand and a breast pocket full of percussion caps.

> *Wars need killin, and I'm the killin kind.*
> *Tell them Jesse is coming, they know the name.*

Here, the teenage face of Death, astride a starving horse, split
the Kansas City fair. They pulled their pockets wide for him.

> *We aint all gonna die easy,*
> *but you aint gotta die hard today.*

How they trembled and panted in the afternoon sun.
How they lathered their bodies with vulgar fables.

River Water

for Beloved

She wants to be outside of
everything. She wants out,
outside of the wanting
mostly. Wanting feels
like a god. She wants
outside of that too.
She wants to be outside
of gods. There is no quiet
like the dead space she is in.

The quiet the body makes
by erasing noise,
the deafness after a gunshot,
the forgetting, the way we can forget.

It is a buzzing quiet, a little motor,
the body makes
when blotting out the sounds of death
or many deaths.

River water
drown her with dreaming.
She can't stay hurt.
The body doesn't hold hurt
like that. The body saves us,
even as we are dying, from the last futile pain.

Finally, wonder.
Wonder remains.

When the Vendor Dies

We will crush bins of herbs and flowers,
leave their parts splayed open,

press petals to our tongues,
lop branches from barren trees.

When the vendor dies, we will break his jars,
scratch ourselves with unforgiving clay,

hold the potter's still warm wheel at dawn,
dash it into the gobbling slash of river.

We will split our nails on his cracked carts,
stop our mouths with his apples' pliant, rotten flesh.

Open, angry river, give us his death to bury.
We will pull oil from his scorched bone.

Tide, be brief; evening swell, clobber us.

In the Beginning, Death

"The man named his wife Eve, because she would become the mother of all the living."

—Genesis 3:20

I enter,
a type of Adam:
        one greasy sparerib
touched by God,
all Amazon (taller, even!),
        approach strident,
lashing his ears like a fallen angel.

Astride an altered ocean
        (*this* is timelessness),
mountainous with salt,
        I look for clear water.
Overhead, the first black nights beat their wings,
        hesitant to fly.

Portable, I'm meager,
a dented can
in God's taxonomy of liabilities.
        Woe.
This should be paradise.

My heart stiffens
        like a moldy rind.
More like God than ever,
I'll plant my son in the ground,
fill cracked jars with water,
        and scrape my way across the sharpened earth.

Lo and behold, as a comet curves
the sooty rim of night,
as one who serves,
I may rest in familiar flights.

Ophelia by Water

Even with the buzz and prick of summer,
what thumped in her brain
was not the pulse of a dark thicket,
the frenetic crescendo of cicadas,
but snippets of verse that sounded sacred.
She turned away from noise,
cooling her hem in the current,
washing a hand over her face.

Lit from within,
she was a candle to the cerulean shadows
perched on the edge
of a black tangle of climbing vines.
She waited, a doll half wooden and half glass.

Later, the sky would shiver under autumn's black hood,
all pinpricked iridescent, cold air floating
in ghostly currents.

All Names Are Curses

You've been whirring
under the cover of ash,
kicking up debris like a stuck wheel.

You've been calling yourself
everything, pressing
the world into your taut center
like a dead star.

It's the way you are pieced together,
barbed-wire spine,
wooden hands,
brine for blood.

One morning you will dream
you are a shuddering moth trapped
behind bluish glass in an abandoned warehouse.

One morning you will wake, blackened doll,
and worry you've been singing your life away.

One morning you will find your heart
is a fish gutted and stinking up a shoreline.

Desire is a different sort of curse.

With no lover to fold into,
this emptied parking lot is an ocean,
white markers rising off the pavement in waves,
grit pricking the bottoms of your feet.

The ache's vibration is a fingerprint
on your small parts.

An Element of Blank (Ophelia Reprise)

Her fingers twitched,
brown twigs. Expect more
from a body that is not yet dead.
If these sheets were snow,
she could have been entirely wooden.

By the sink a straight razor winked,
having dark visions.

Night swelled while she shrank.

Everyday griefs multiplied,
vines in a wretched, lush garden.

In the frozen yard, leafless trees filed away;
a spider hitched black insect legs
to a broken net.
Catching electric light,
a slick leaf flickered
like an erratic butterfly.

Rain approached in
a silent sky.

Though she waited for night to whisper something tragic,
she would not incline her head.

Acknowledgments

Many thanks to the following publications for publishing earlier versions of the following poems:

"Cinderella Sends Her Godmother Away," "Song, without a Musical Note for My Granddaddy," and "Intersection" were published in *Callaloo* 34.4.

"Uncle Bubba's Funeral" published in *Cave Canem Anthology XII*.

"Judas Kiss," "Last Lament for Judas," and "The Temptation of Saint Anthony" were published in *New England Review* 32.2.

"The Palm Beach Story," "The Florida Motel," and "Leaping Fire in Princeville Park" are forthcoming from *Poetry Northwest*.

"Naked, in a Stormy Passage" was published in *Southern Humanities Review* 49.3.

"Certain Immutable Laws" and "What Might Not Break Through" were published in *Valley Voices* 11.1.

So much of this work began and was shaped by the poets and professors in my MFA program at the University of Florida. Thank you to Sidney Wade and Michael Hofmann. Tremendous gratitude to my advisors, William Logan and Debora Greger; without your sincere and gracious attention these poems would not have been written. William, you are my first and greatest teacher of poetry.

Warm and unyielding gratitude to Cave Canem as an organization that champions great poetry and as a family of some of my greatest champions. Thank you especially to all the faculty who read my work and gave me feedback: Cyrus Cassells, Toi Derricotte, Cornelius Eady, Terrance Hayes, Yusef Kumunyakaa, Colleen J. McElroy, Carl Phillips, Claudia Rankine, Ed Robeson, Patricia Smith, and Natasha Tretheway. This list of names is incredibly humbling. Thank you for your voice, your work, and your suggestions. Thank you fellows, F. Douglas Brown, Jericho Brown, Mahogany Brown, Nandi Comer, Robin Coste-Lewis, DeLana R. A. Dameron, Aricka Forman, Jonterri Gadson, Deidre Gantt, francine j. harris, JP Howard, Ashaki Jackson, Amanda Johnston, Bettina Judd, Dante Micheaux, Rachel Nelson, Cedric Tillman, Anastacia Tolbert,

Qiana Towns, Maya Washington, and L. Lamar Wilson; so many of you, and so many others, held me and my poems up to the light.

Thank you again and again, Kwame Dawes for selecting my collection. Your poems are essential and lovely. I'm deeply honored that you chose mine.

Thank you to Jack Jones Literary Arts and Kima Jones for your unwavering advocacy for writers.

Thank you to my Cal State Fullerton friends in life and poetry: Thank you, Jie Tian—how absolutely peerless is your thoughtfulness. Thank you, Irena Praitis, for welcoming me into the space you make for poetry. Erica Ball, Sonia Velez, the Ethnic Studies Department, and College of Humanities and Social Sciences, thank you.

Thank you to my family of friends: Thank you, Julie and Kinney Barbour, you are pillars that hold my son and I aloft. Kourtney and Kelcie Barbour, how lucky I am to watch you grow into your magic. Janelle Rahyns and Tina Taylor Allison for your honest loyalty. Keetje Kuipers, I love how and that our lives unfold together. Kelly Myers-Musset, your intellect inspires me. Fletcher MCCloud, working overtime, late nights, and early mornings, heavy, heavy love. Cynthia A. Briano, always, for everything you spin into joy, I love you. Pero Dagbovie, Johnnie Eiland, Gina Galassi, and Daniel Mahfood for your persistent faith, and support.

Thank you to the Woods, Grahams, and Mitchells for every kindness. Thank you, Nate; you are a true creative genius. Latechia, you are my best friend and anchor always. Randolph, continue to nurture your desire for right. Joelle, you are a princess. RKIII, you are the best part of everything I do. Dad, thank you for your encouragement along this journey. And Mom, I miss you terribly and love you—words fail these feelings.

CPSIA information can be obtained
at www.ICGtesting.com
Printed in the USA
LVHW04s2335240718
584769LV00001B/20/P